For all portable keyboards.

THE COMPLETE
KEYBOARD PLAYER
PICTURE CHORDS

Exclusive distributors:

Hal Leonard
7777 West Bluemound Road, Milwaukee, WI 53213
Email: info@halleonard.com

Hal Leonard Europe Limited
42 Wigmore Street Maryleborne, London, WIU 2 RN
Email: info@halleonardeurope.com

Hal Leonard Australia Pty. Ltd.
4 Lentara Court Cheltenham, Victoria, 9132 Australia
Email: info@halleonard.com.au

Order No. AM89542

ISBN 0.7119.3041.4

Thihs book © Copyright by Hal Leonard

Book design by Studio Twenty, London
Music processed by The Pitts

Printed in EU.

www.halleonard.com

Layout of the keyboard

Your electronic keyboard looks something like this:-

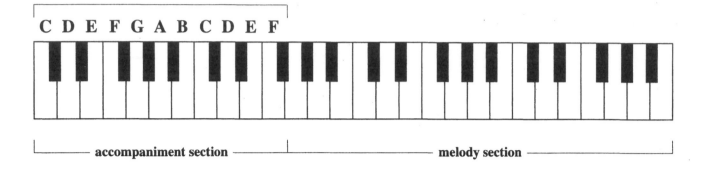

The left hand section of the keyboard is used for the **accompaniment.**

The remainder of the keyboard is used for the **melody.**

Fingered chords

Some keyboards allow you to play single-finger chords, where you press one key and a full chord sounds. However, all the chords in this book are fingered chords, which means that you play all the notes in the chord.

Switch on your keyboard and select 'fingered chords' (refer to your owner's manual).

In the 'accompaniment' section of your keyboard, play the following three notes together:-

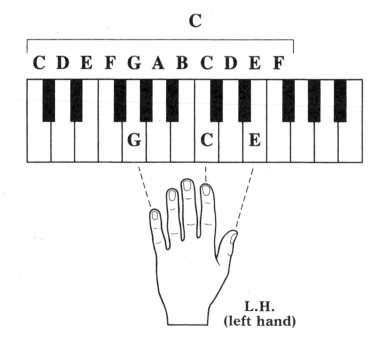

This time you should be hearing, and actually playing a chord of C.

Finger numbers

In this book we have suggested left hand fingerings for each chord.

Your fingers are numbered from 1 to 5, like this:-

Your left hand plays the accompaniment.

Your right hand plays the melody.

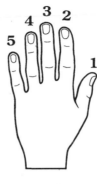

L.H.
(left hand)

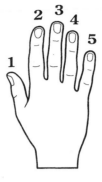

R.H.
(right hand)

Chord inversions

To make the chords sound good on the keyboard, often they must be played with the notes slightly rearranged into what are known as *inversions*. You will come to learn these chords by their basic sounds, even if the inversion has changed or some notes have been dropped out.

We have provided the picture chords with the most appropriate inversions for a keyboard with a left hand accompaniment. If you have a piano you will be able to play the chords in all their inversions.

| C Maj triad | 1st Inversion | 2nd Inversion | C Maj (with 3rd dropped out) | C7 | 2nd Inversion | (tonic drops out) |

Simple chord progressions

Music is described as being in a 'key'. The key is defined by the scale it relates to and its primary chords. These are always the chords on the first, fourth and fifth degrees of the scale (e.g. in the key of C they would be the chords of C, F and G).

All keys are related around a *cycle of fifths.*

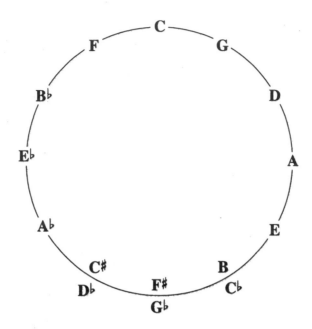

If you look at the drawing you will see that each key is related to the next by 5 notes, and if we played each key in sequence around the cycle we would arrive back at C.

The notes in a scale can be numbered in roman numerals:-

I II III IV V VI VII I

Scale of C major

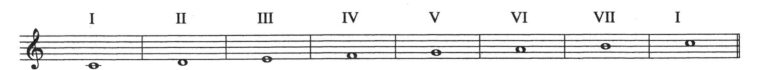

I, IV, and V are primary or strong chords and there are many progressions which include these three chords, including the ending of pieces.

You can start anywhere, but your first move determines your key. If you start with a chord of C as I, then F and G must be the other primary chords. If you started with A as I, then D and E would be the other primary chords.

We can make the chords sound more interesting by adding the 7th.

The most common use of the primary chords in rock and pop music is the 12-bar blues. We can rearrange the chords to give a simple blues progression:-

I I I I IV IV I I V IV I I

in the key of C

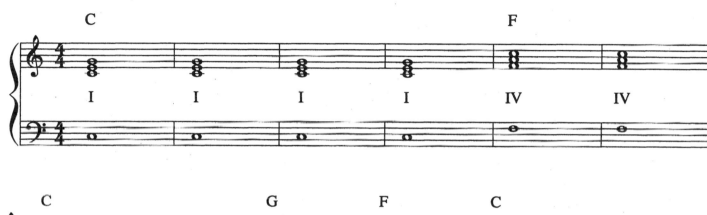

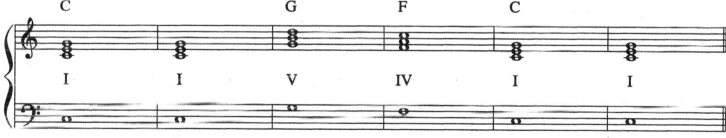

in the key of A

You can experiment with the 12-bar blues progression by playing it in any key of your choice, as long as you remember that the note you choose for chord I dictates the IV and V chords.

C

accompaniment section

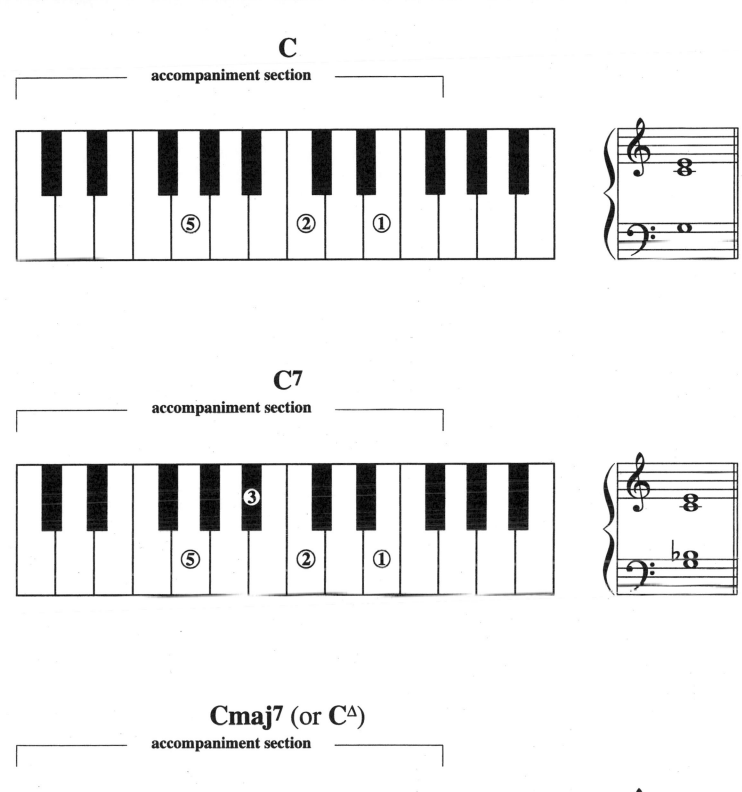

C7

accompaniment section

Cmaj7 (or C△)

accompaniment section

C6

accompaniment section

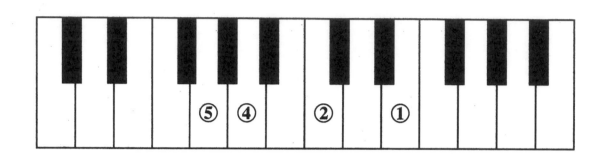

Csus4

accompaniment section

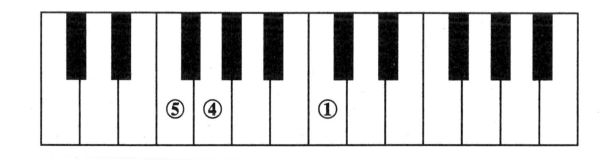

C7sus4

accompaniment section

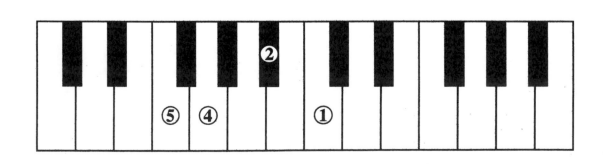

Caug (or C+)

accompaniment section

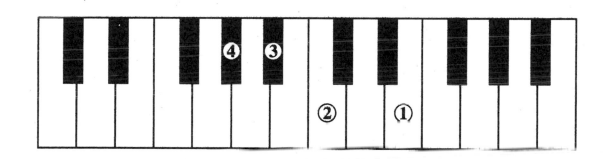

C7#5 (or C7+)

accompaniment section

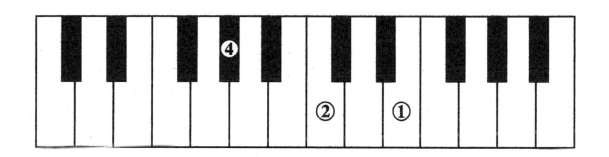

Cm

accompaniment section

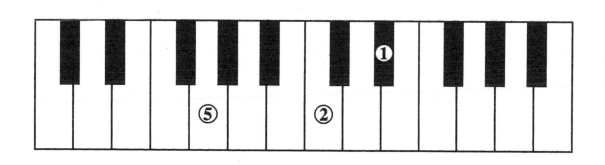

The C Collection

Cm7

accompaniment section

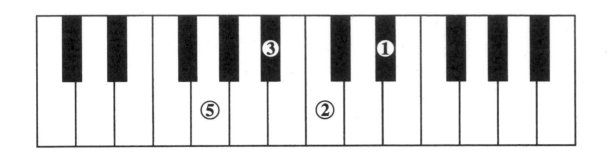

Cdim (or C°)

accompaniment section

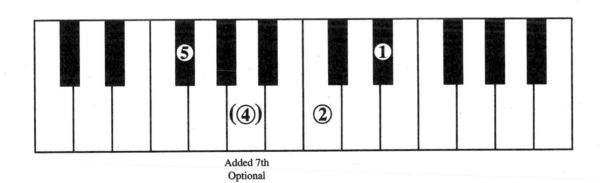

Added 7th
Optional

Cm7(♭5) (or CØ)

accompaniment section

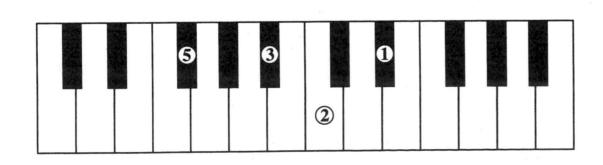

The D♭ Collection

D♭

accompaniment section

D♭7

accompaniment section

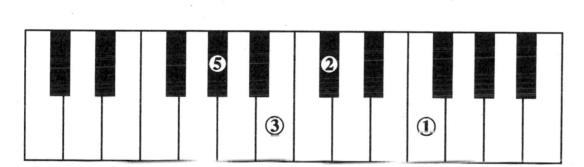

D♭maj7 (or D♭△)

accompaniment section

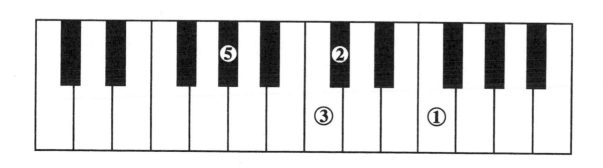

The D♭ Collection

D♭6

accompaniment section

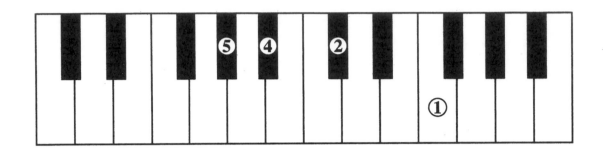

D♭sus4

accompaniment section

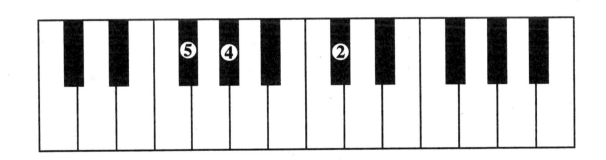

D♭7sus4

accompaniment section

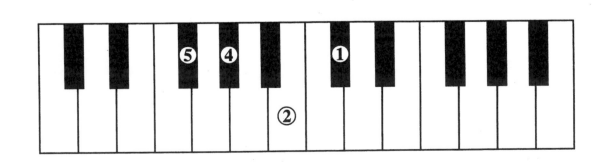

14

D♭aug (or D♭+)

accompaniment section

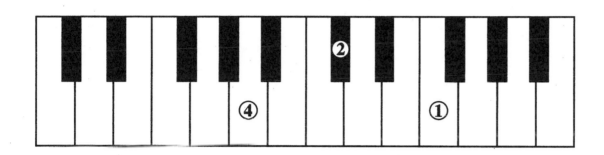

D♭7#5

accompaniment section

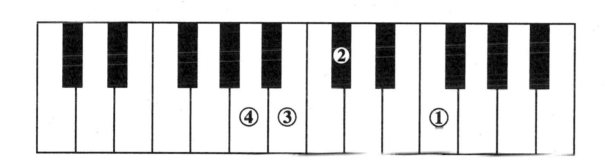

C♯m or D♭m

accompaniment section

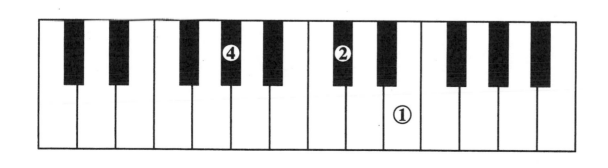

C#m7 or D♭m7

accompaniment section

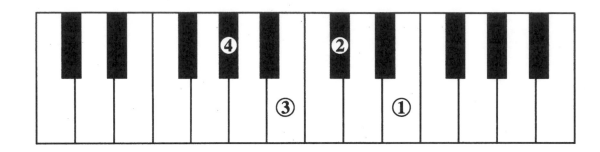

C#dim or D♭dim (C#°/D♭°)

accompaniment section

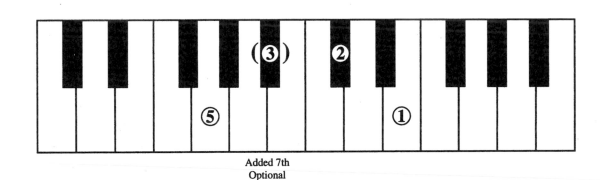

Added 7th
Optional

C#m7(♭5) or D♭m7(♭5) (C#m7(-5)/D♭m7(-5))

accompaniment section

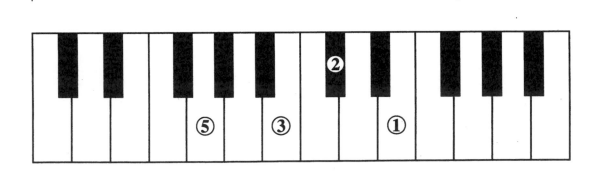

D

accompaniment section

D7

accompaniment section

Dmaj7 (or D△)

accompaniment section

The D Collection

D6

accompaniment section

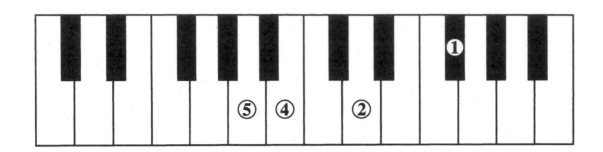

Dsus4

accompaniment section

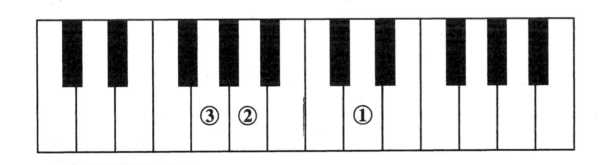

D7sus4

accompaniment section

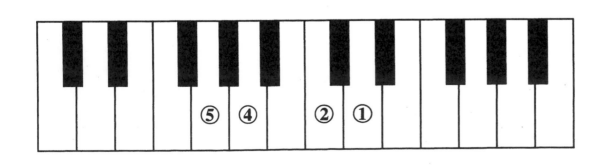

Daug (or D⁺)

Daug (or **D⁺**)

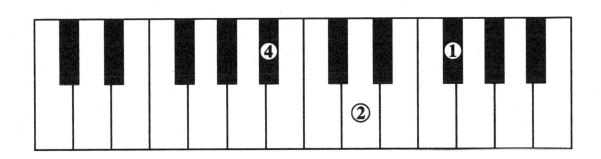

D7(♯5) (or **D7⁺**)

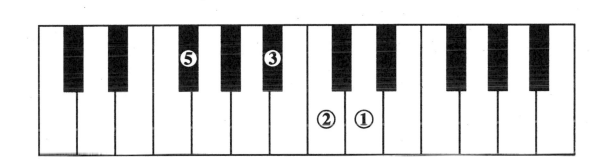

Dm

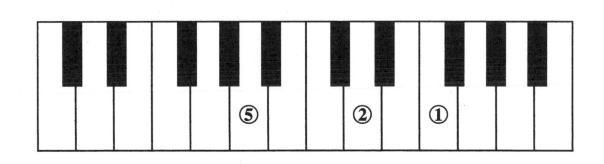

The D Collection

Dm7

accompaniment section

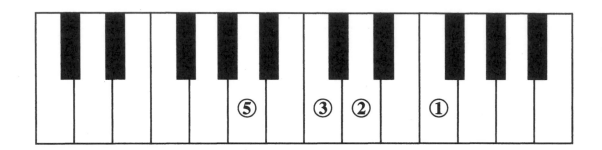

Ddim (or D°)

accompaniment section

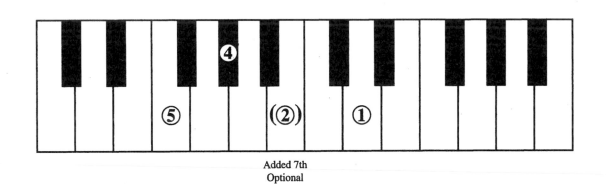

Added 7th
Optional

Dm7(♭5) (or D∅)

accompaniment section

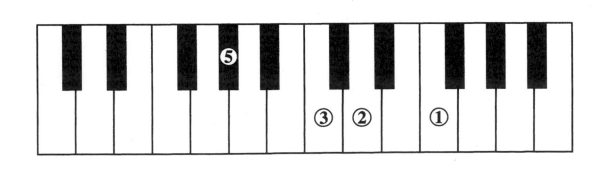

E♭

accompaniment section

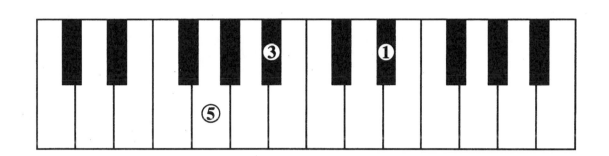

E♭7

accompaniment section

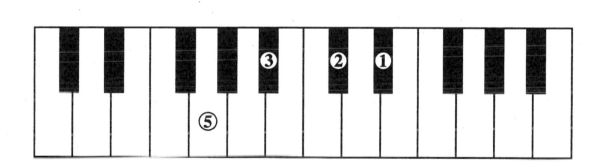

E♭maj7 (or E♭△)

accompaniment section

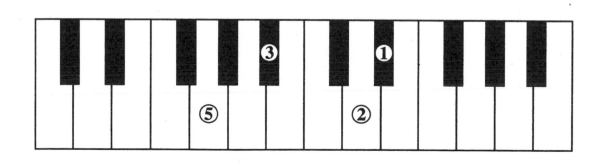

E♭6

accompaniment section

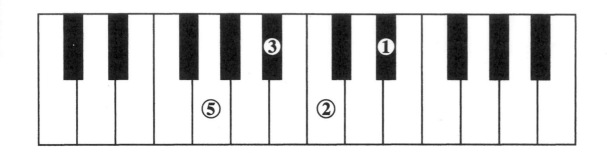

E♭sus4

accompaniment section

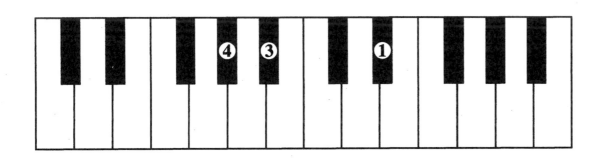

E♭7sus4

accompaniment section

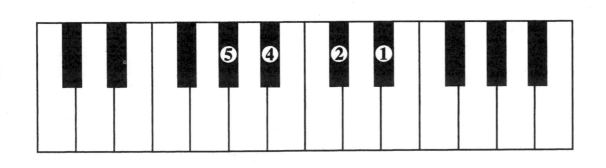

E♭aug(E♭+)

accompaniment section

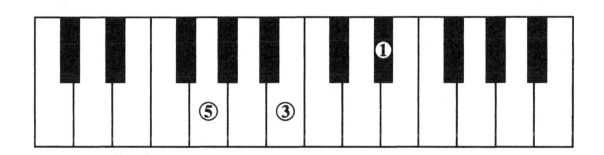

E♭7(♯5) (or E♭7+)

accompaniment section

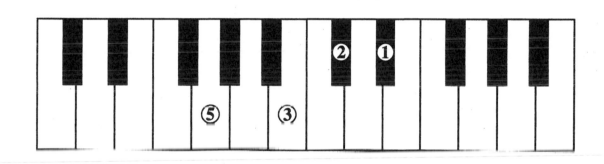

E♭m

accompaniment section

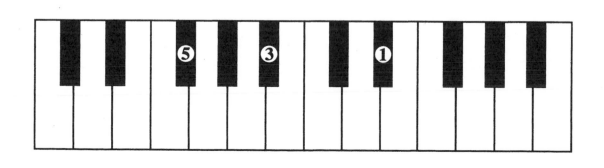

23

E♭m7

accompaniment section

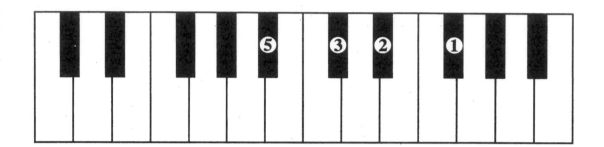

E♭dim (or E♭°)

accompaniment section

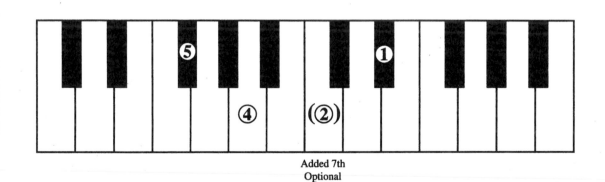

Added 7th
Optional

E♭m7(♭5) (or E♭ø)

accompaniment section

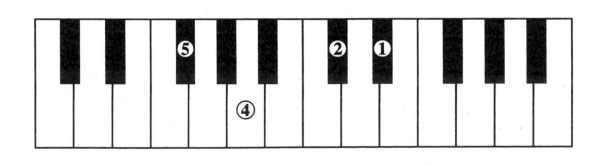

E

accompaniment section

E7

accompaniment section

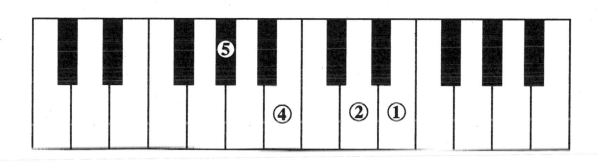

Emaj7 (or E△)

accompaniment section

The E Collection

E6

accompaniment section

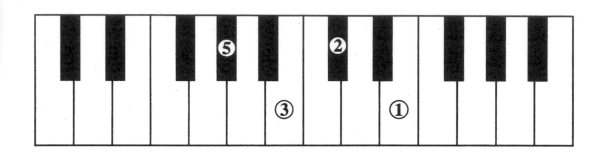

Esus4

accompaniment section

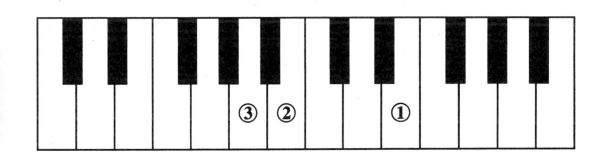

E7sus4

accompaniment section

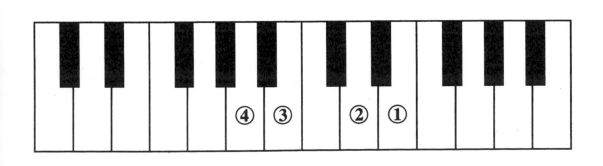

Eaug (or E+)

accompaniment section

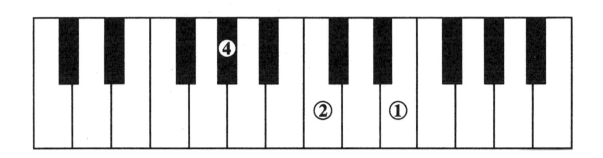

E7(♯5) (or E7+)

accompaniment section

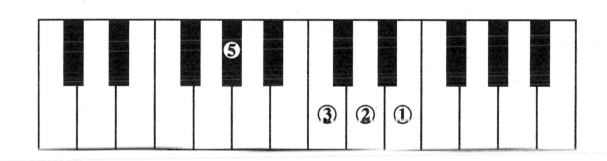

Em

accompaniment section

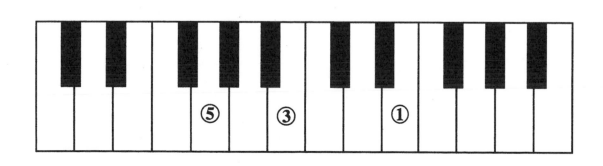

Em7

accompaniment section

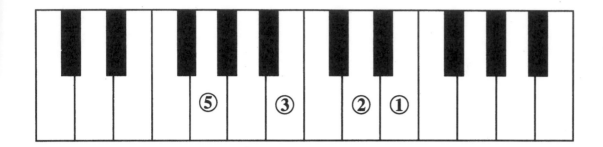

Edim (or E°)

accompaniment section

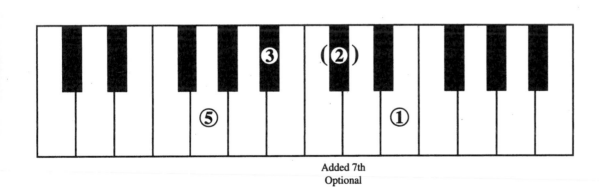

Added 7th
Optional

Em7(♭5) (or Eø)

accompaniment section

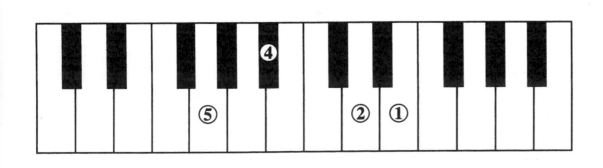

The F Collection

F

accompaniment section

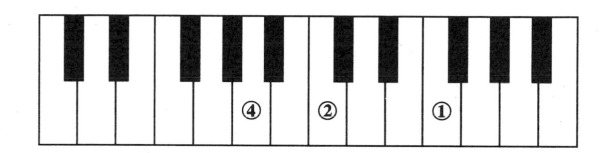

F7

accompaniment section

Fmaj7 (or F△)

accompaniment section

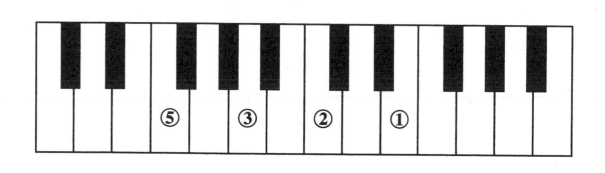

The F Collection

F6

accompaniment section

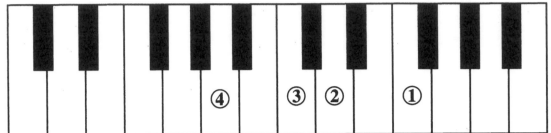

Fsus⁴

accompaniment section

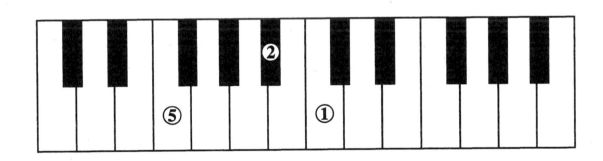

F⁷sus⁴

accompaniment section

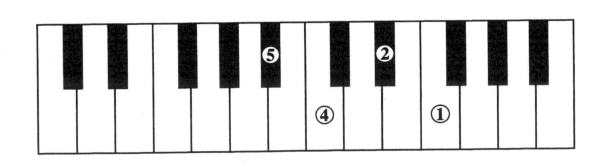

Faug (or F⁺)

accompaniment section

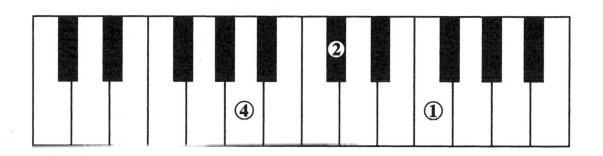

F7(♯5) (or F7⁺)

accompaniment section

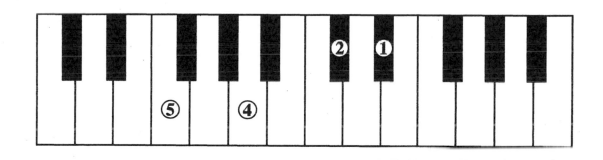

Fm

accompaniment section

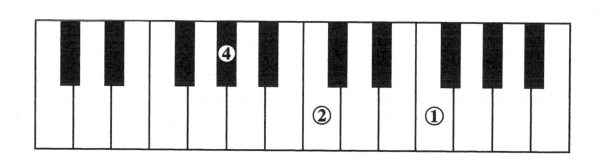

The F Collection

Fm7

accompaniment section

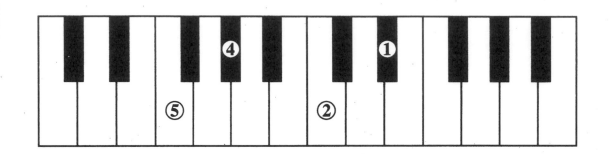

Fdim (or F°)

accompaniment section

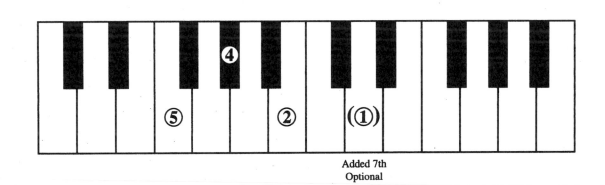

Added 7th
Optional

Fm7(♭5) (or Fø)

accompaniment section

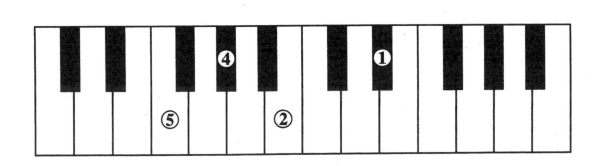
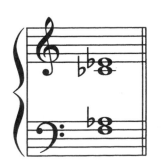

The G♭ Collection

G♭

accompaniment section

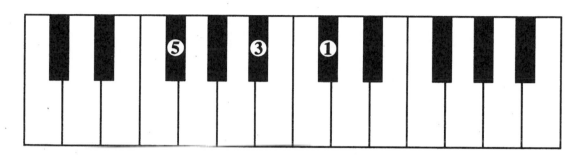

G♭7

accompaniment section

G♭maj7 (or G♭△)

accompaniment section

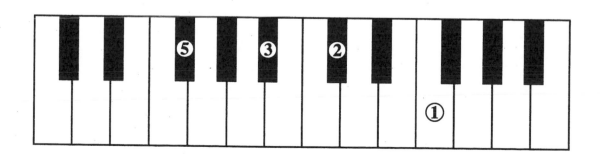

G♭6

accompaniment section

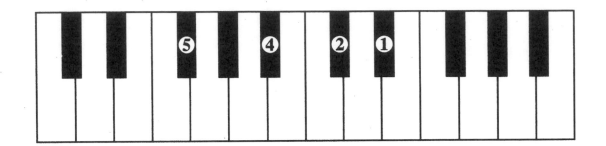

G♭sus4

accompaniment section

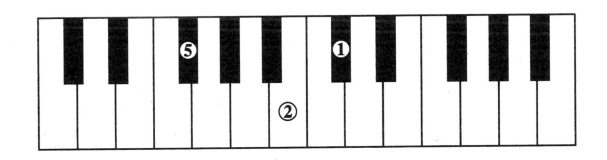

G♭7sus4

accompaniment section

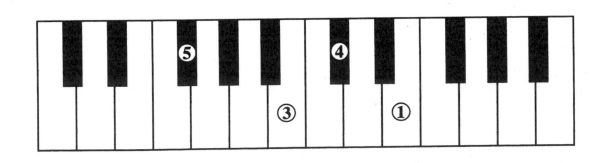

G♭aug (or G♭+)

accompaniment section

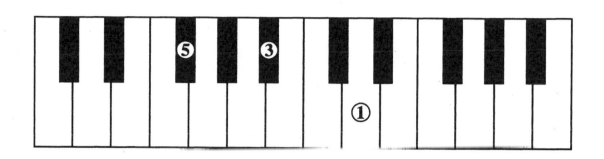

G♭7(♯5) (or G♭7+)

accompaniment section

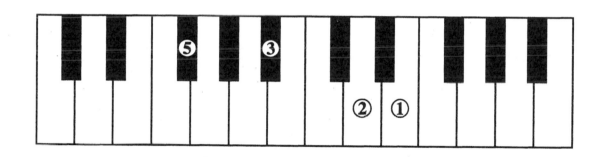

F♯m

accompaniment section

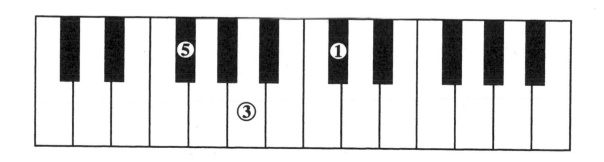

F#m7

accompaniment section

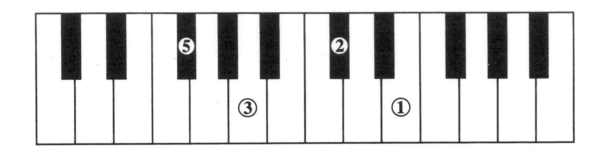

F#dim (or F#°)

accompaniment section

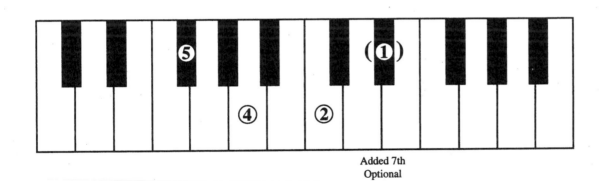

Added 7th
Optional

F#m7(♭5) (or F#∅)

accompaniment section

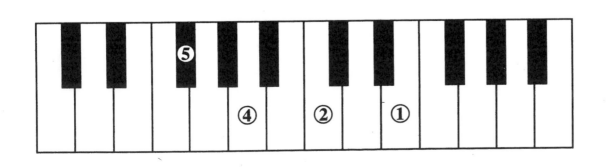

The G Collection

G

accompaniment section

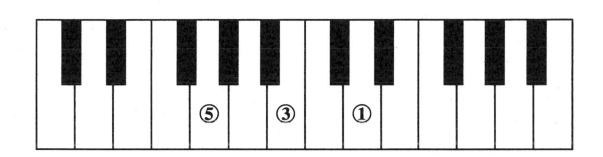

G7

accompaniment section

Gmaj7 (or G^Δ)

accompaniment section

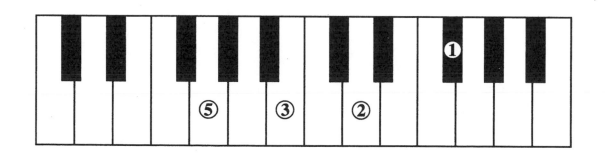

The G Collection

G6

accompaniment section

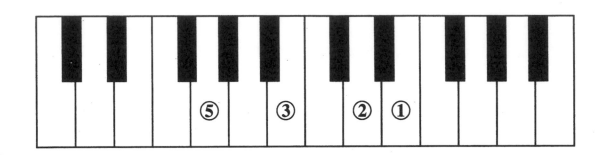

Gsus4

accompaniment section

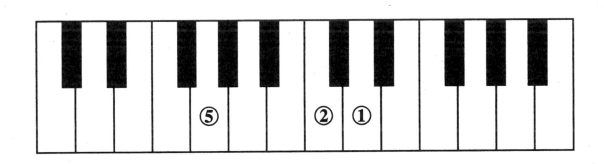

G7sus4

accompaniment section

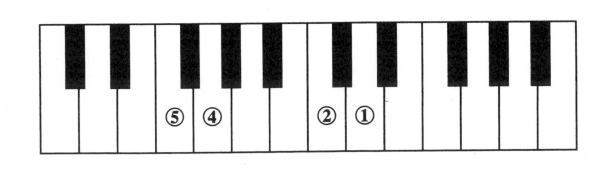

Gaug (or G⁺)

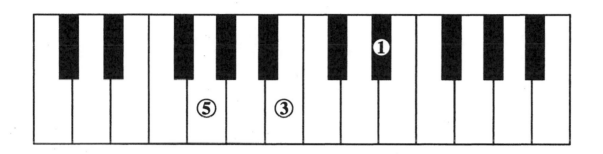

G7(♯5) (or G7⁺)

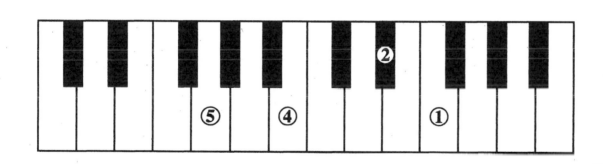

Gm

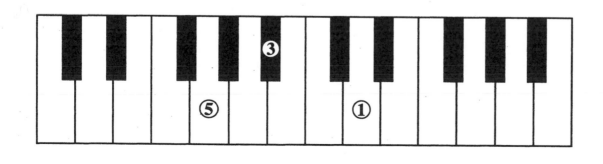

The G Collection

Gm7

accompaniment section

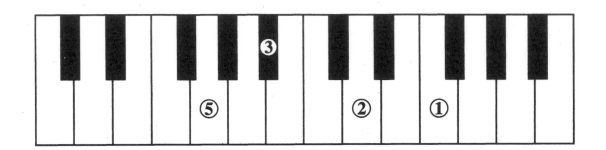

Gdim (or G°)

accompaniment section

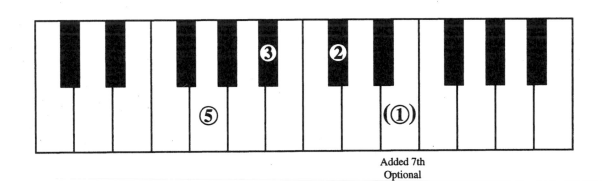

Added 7th
Optional

Gm7(♭5) (or G∅)

accompaniment section

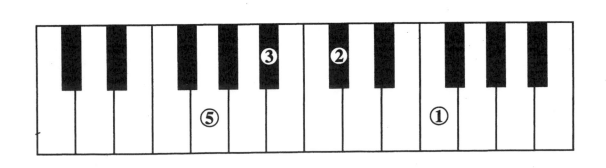

The A♭ Collection

A♭

accompaniment section

A♭7

accompaniment section

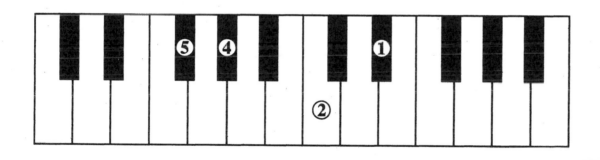

A♭maj7 (or A♭△)

accompaniment section

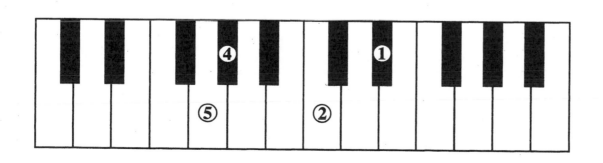

The A♭ Collection

A♭6

accompaniment section

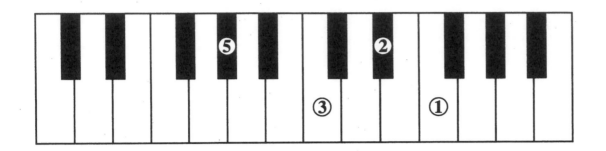

A♭sus4

accompaniment section

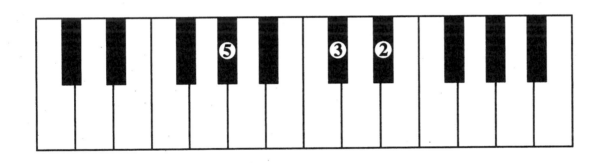

A♭7sus4

accompaniment section

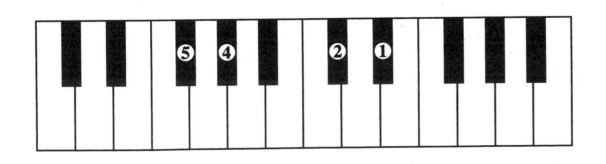

A♭aug (or A♭+)

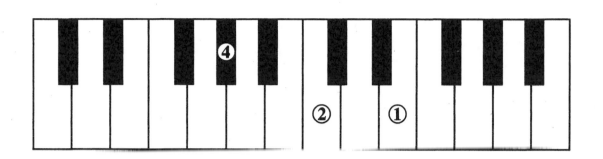

A♭7(♯5) (or A♭7+)

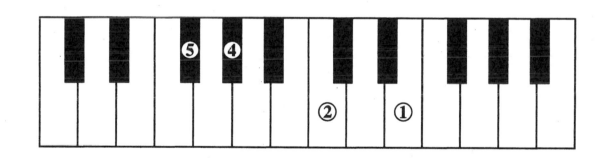

G♯m

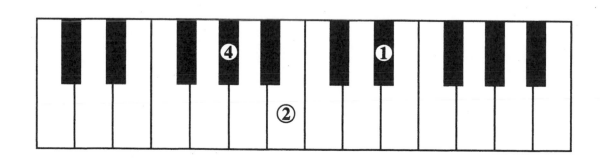

G#m7

accompaniment section

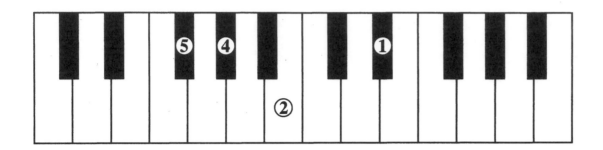

G#dim (or G#°)

accompaniment section

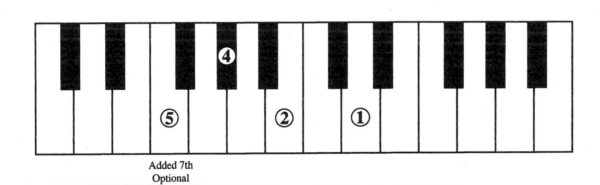

Added 7th
Optional

G#m7(♭5) (or G#ø)

accompaniment section

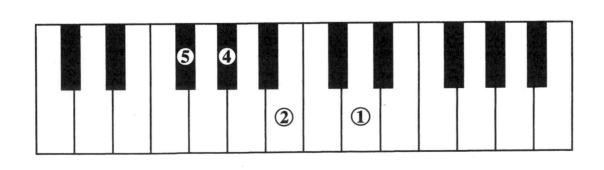

The A Collection

A

accompaniment section

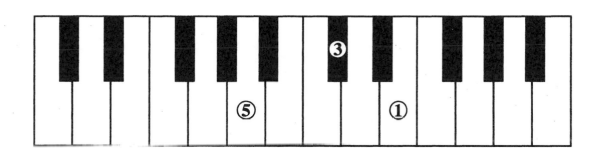

A7

accompaniment section

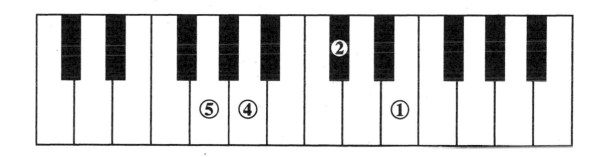

Amaj7 (or A△)

accompaniment section

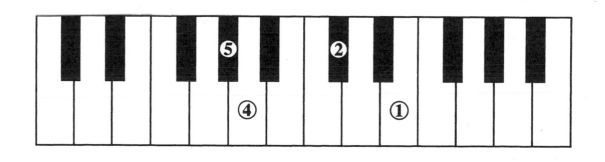

The A Collection

A6

accompaniment section

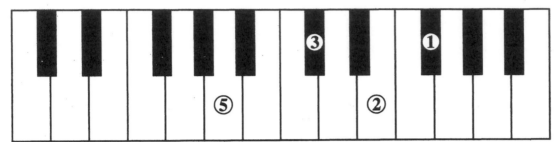

Asus4

accompaniment section

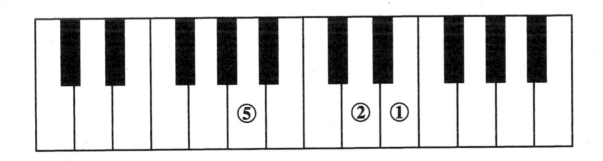

A7sus4

accompaniment section

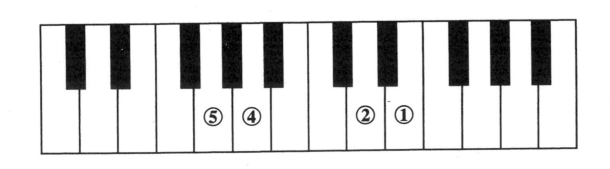

Aaug (or A⁺)

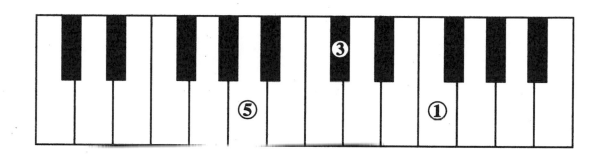

A7(♯5) (or A7⁺)

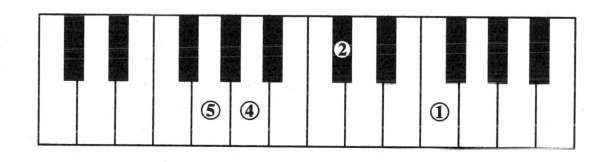

Am

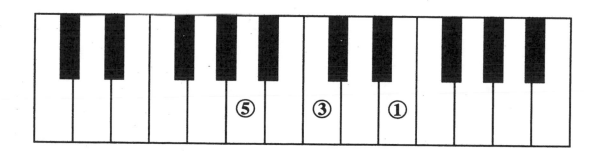

The A Collection

Am7

accompaniment section

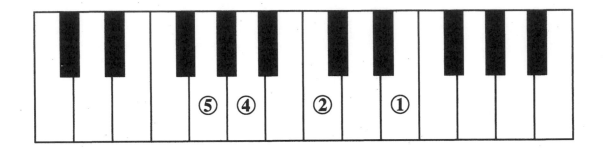

Adim (or A°)

accompaniment section

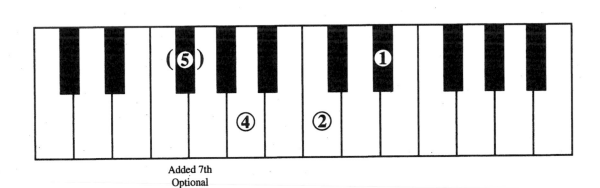

Added 7th
Optional

Am7(♭5) (or Aø)

accompaniment section

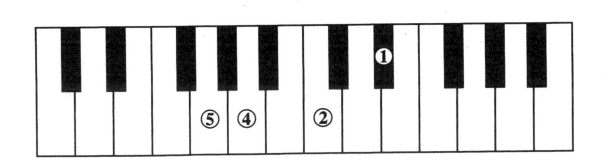

The B♭ Collection

B♭

accompaniment section

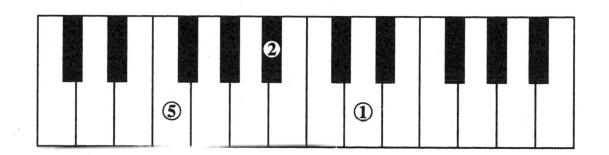

B♭7

accompaniment section

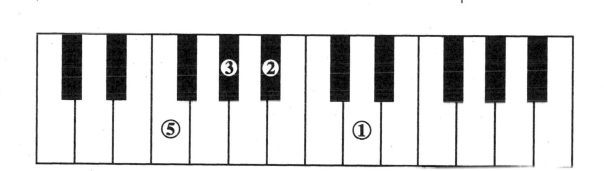

B♭maj7 (or B♭△)

accompaniment section

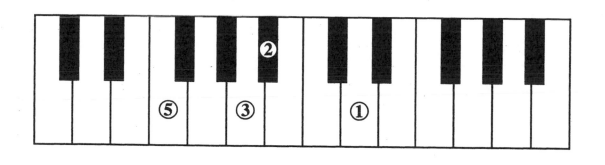

The B♭ Collection

B♭6

accompaniment section

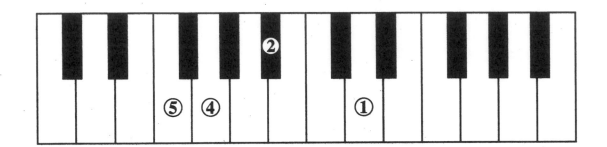

B♭sus4

accompaniment section

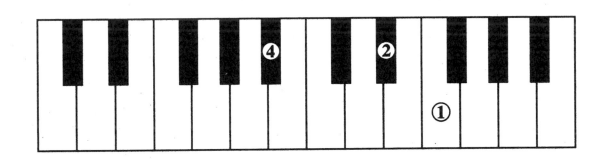

B♭7sus4

accompaniment section

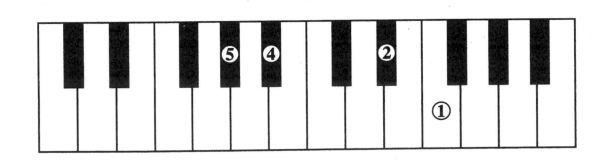

B♭aug (or B♭+)

accompaniment section

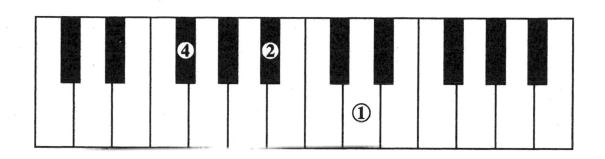

B♭7(♯5) (or B♭+)

accompaniment section

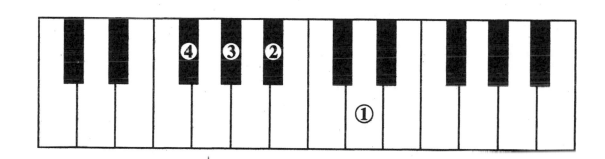

B♭m

accompaniment section

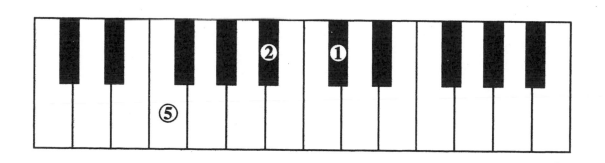

B♭m7

accompaniment section

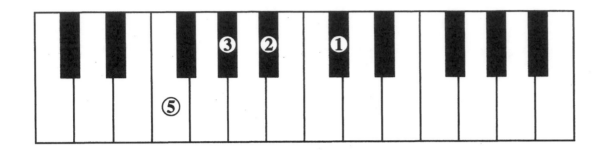

B♭dim (or B♭°)

accompaniment section

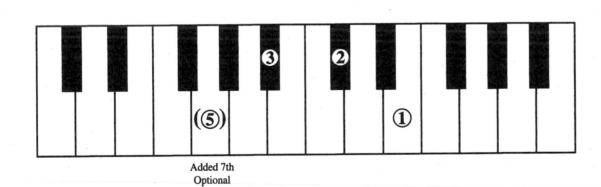

Added 7th
Optional

B♭m7(♭5) (or B♭ø)

accompaniment section

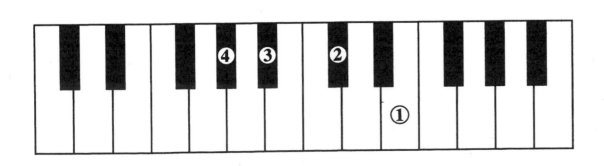

B

accompaniment section

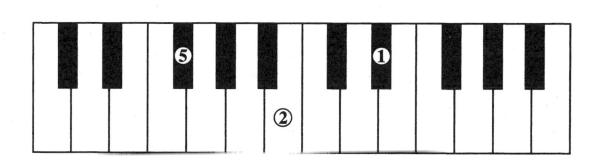

B7

accompaniment section

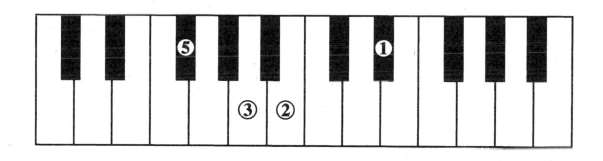

Bmaj7 (or B△)

accompaniment section

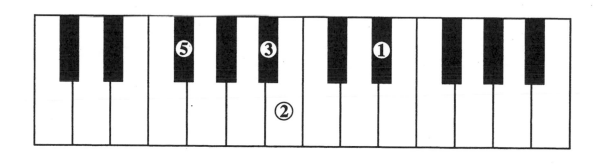

The B Collection

B6

accompaniment section

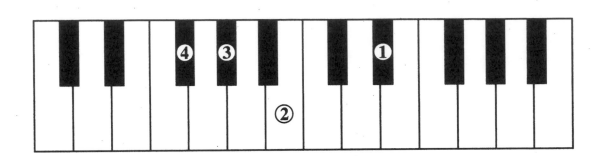

Bsus4

accompaniment section

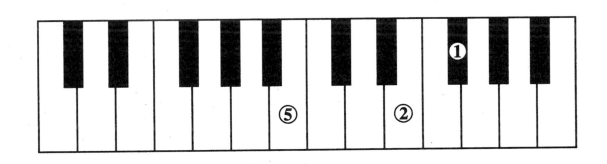

B7sus4

accompaniment section

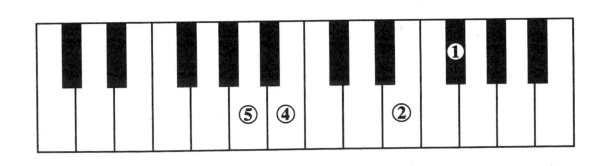

Baug (or B⁺)

accompaniment section

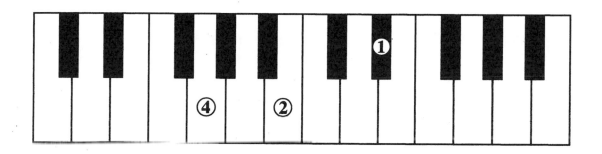

B7(♯5) (or B7⁺)

accompaniment section

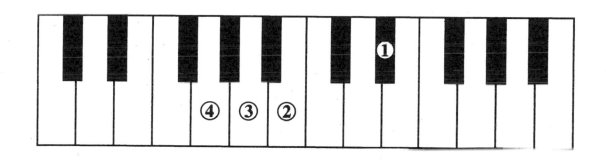

Bm

accompaniment section

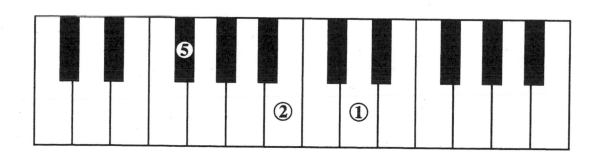

The B Collection

Bm7

accompaniment section

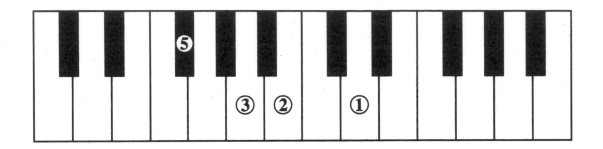

Bdim (or B°)

accompaniment section

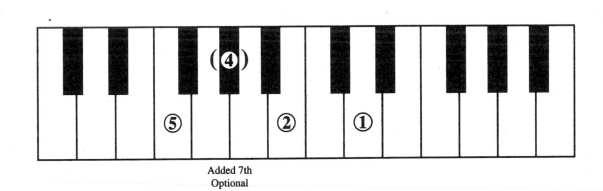

Added 7th
Optional

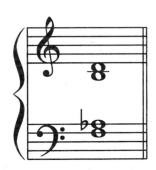

Bm7(♭5) (or Bᴓ)

accompaniment section

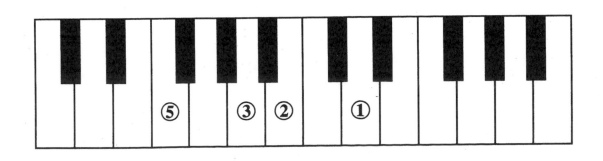